Sloth Bear!

An Animal Encyclopedia for Kids (Bear Kingdom)

Children's Biological Science of Bears Books

PRODIGYWIZARD
BOOKS

LET'S GET TO KNOW THIS AMAZING CREATURE – THE SLOTH BEAR.
SLOTH BEARS ARE KNOWN TO BE NOCTURNAL AND NOISY ANIMALS.

Have you met one? Well, most probably. If you've watched a the movie Ice Age, you may have seen a sloth bear.

Have you read Rudyard Kipling's The Jungle Book? One of the characters is Baloo, who is a sloth bear.

Sloth bears are usually active at night and sleep during the day. They are considered nocturnal. But in protected areas, some can be active during the day.

They are very noisy. They snort and grunt while looking for food by pulling out branches to get twigs to dig for termites.

Sloth bears use their lips to vacuum insects. When they do this, they produce a loud noise. Sloth bears usually wander alone in the forests looking for food.

PHYSICAL DESCRIPTION

Sloth bears have long, shaggy, black fur coats. Their fur looks very messy.

They have long curved claws they use to get ants and termites. They have long, pale-colored snouts and bare lips.

They have cream- colored "V" or "Y" designs on their chests. Their nostrils close, protecting them from dust while they search for and excavate ants.

Sloth bears' teeth have gaps which allow them to suck up insects and termites.

SIZE

Sloth bears can grow to five to six feet, or 1.8 meters, in length. They can stand two to three feet high at the shoulder.

Male sloth bears weigh up to 140 kilograms or 310 pounds. Lighter females can weigh up to 95 kilograms or 210 pounds.

GEOGRAPHIC DISTRIBUTION

Most of sloth bears' population can be found in India and Sri Lanka. Other sloth bears live in Southern Nepal, Bhutan, and Bangladesh.

HABITAT

Sloth bears live in hot jungles. They sleep in caves but they don't hibernate.

It's warm. They never have to deal with snow or cold, so there's no need to have a long winter sleep.

REPRODUCTION

The female sloth bear gets pregnant for six to seven months. The female sloth bears usually give birth to two cubs. They do this in an underground den.

The cubs stay with their mother for two to three years before they become independent.

Sloth bears are ready to bear babies when they are two or three years old.

DIET: THE OMNIVORES.

Sloth bears mainly feed themselves on ants and termites, so their diet is insect-based.

They suck up insects and termites using their lips. They have no incisor teeth.

But if fruits are in season, sloth bears love to eat fruit. They also dine on some flowers.

Sloth bears also knock down honeycombs and dine on the honey. During a food shortage, sloth bears raid fields and eat the crops.

PREDATORS

Young sloth bears are in danger from tigers, wolves and leopards, but their main predators are humans.

People hunt sloth bears for their gall bladders, which are used in eastern medicine.

IT'S SAD TO NOTE THAT HUMANS ARE PART OF THE REDUCTION OF SLOTH BEARS. IS THERE SOMETHING WE CAN DO TO HELP THEM?

WHAT DO YOU THINK?

CPSIA information can be obtained
at www.ICGtesting.com
Printed in the USA
LVHW061054090920
665432LV00015B/1189

9 781683 239710